The Comeback's Exoskeleton

poems

Matthew Rotando

 UpSet Press, Inc.
P.O. Box 200340
Brooklyn, NY 11220
www.upsetpress.org

Copyright © 2008 by Matthew Rotando.
All poems written by Matthew Rotando,
except "Tournament of Nakedness,"
by Matthew Rotando and Alicia Marie Howard.
Cover art: "The Sloth and La Pachamama,"
by Gregory Ferrand. (www. gferrand.com)
Cover and text design by Aaron Kenedi.

UpSet Press is an open and supportive space for artists who offer new visions in written language. The press produces mainly first books and newly revised editions of exceptional out-of-print books. Founded in 2000 by a group of NYC-based poets, the press publishes SPAWN'zine, conducts regular poetry workshops, and group readings around the city. In 2005, UpSet Press published *Theater of War*, a collection of poetry and political satire by Nicholas Powers.

First printing, April 2008
ISBN 978-0-9760142-1-8
Printed in the United States of America
10 9 8 7 6 5 4 3 2 1

*for my grandparents and parents
and for Todd*

Contents

I. Lions And Geckoes

II. Regular Stuff

III. A Good Fall

Foreword

THE TITLE, *The Comeback's Exoskeleton,* has the air of a paradox, a receding riddle you can't quite get your mind around. I mean, wow, it's really something to think about. Matthew Rotando has written a puzzling, radiant book in which surprise, generosity, and openness are watching martial arts movies together late into the night. Incorporating the density of Spanish surrealism and a sprawling Whitmanesque line, this amazing first book finds Rotando engaged in a poetic biathlon which draws equally from maximal and minimal traditions. There are tight, economical poems, free verse forms derived from the sonnet, poems leaping about the page, but my favorites are the wonderful prose poems tumbling over and under themselves toward gnomish statements that feel both didactic and self-parodying. Rotando's poems float in a meditative atmosphere which disperses the subject speaking, and in this situation, the meditative turn inward becomes a paradoxical opening up to the world.

This poetry feels timely in its use of tone and affect, and it achieves that without resorting to irony, camp, or kitsch. No archness, coyness, or nastiness here. On the contrary, Rotando's humor comes from a constant sense of surprise via transmissions from elsewhere, constant unexpected shifts in noun or location enacted by a Candide-like, gee-whiz speaker. Whereas Ashbery's deadpan persona may have been sneering slightly when he wrote "she approached me about buying her desk," Rotando will assert that "We Long For Regular Stuff" and genuinely mean it, in an expansive sense, like a title out of Wallace Stevens. These wan Stevensian riddles are fleshed out by an interest in the material word as grotesque, multisyllabic, and heteroglossic. What results is a goofy, garrulous, embarrassed eagerness: "Ho! Ho! Pond Consonant Boy, look at you, handclapping for bottles and vowels and cans!"

Maybe Rotando is making colloquial speech elegant by using it to surprise: "You, of the mighty darting limbs and bug-bellied singing, I root for you." Maybe he's creating a new kind of affect by mashing together self-consciousness and guilelessness. After all, we know the transmissions from Mars when we receive them, right? At times the work is layered with a sense of mildly amused befuddlement. The poet confides, "I have this feeling, that I have lived too many lives to represent myself honestly. Feel scattered when I try. You feel something, think it's me, be that for a while. We'll both feel freaked when it alters." The clipped, clunky Kerouac syntax of these lines, like Tarzan in therapy, indicates several ways in which "the look the ape gives us is reminiscent of breakfast in the tropics." Rotando's poetry repeatedly enacts the writer's staging of feeling freaked, an enactment foregrounded by that word "weird." Rotando is sensitive to all the ways in which language can feel weird inside the body: "All along the last few steps, I was aware of the way my intestines glooped and glomped." Like a late beatnik pedaling up to you at the Critical Mass bike rally, the poems are suddenly grabbing the addressee by the shoulder and saying "Check it out, man!" And we try, but we can't ever quite figure out what "it" might refer to. What remains instead is a sense of urgent attention to language, antennae quivering as we discover belatedly that we have accidentally put the wrong shoes on the wrong feet and that something consequently feels a little off: "deep deep deep deep deep deep deep cavernous stuff that's dark but bright." Matthew Rotando's poetry understands that Mars is in us. I hope you enjoy his gloriously weird work as much as I do.

Tim Peterson
New York, November 2007

Acknowledgments

I GRATEFULLY acknowledge the editors and publishers of the following journals, in which these poems first appeared:

Eoagh: "Night Of The Reformed Pirate"

BigCityLit.com: "Chant Down Mighty," "Anatomía" and "Anatomy"

The Island (Sri Lanka): "My Thief Went Riding"

Wavelength Magazine: "There's a Fire in my Vitals, Said Old Widow"

"All One And Alone," was selected by Ann Lauterbach as a winner of the Margaret Sterling Prize, offered in 2004 by the University of Arizona Poetry Center.

"Story Of Learning" was selected by Srikanth Reddy as the winner of the Academy of American Poets Prize, offered in 2007 by the University of Arizona Poetry Center.

I offer my sincere thanks to Marlow Daly-Galeano for wonderful editorial assistance on all of the Spanish poems. I'm gratefully indebted to Tim Peterson for his inspiration, advice, and all the fun we had reading poems late into the night at Tucson's Grill Restaurant. I thank Julie Agoos, Lou Asekoff, Richard Pearse, and Carey Harrison for their invaluable help at the beginning of my writing life (where I hope I still am). I thank Master Jen-Chun and Bhikkhu Bodhi for allowing me a short retreat at Bodhi Monastery of Lafayette, New Jersey, where "Story Of Learning" came about.

Deep gratitude also goes to the many friends I made in Sri Lanka who were a great inspiration while I began work on this manuscript, supported by a grant from the Fulbright Foundation.

Hoy nuestros cuerpos se hicieron extensos,
crecieron hasta el límite del mundo
y rodaron fundiéndose
en una sola gota
de cera o meteoro.

Today our bodies became vast,
grew to the edge of the world
and rolled melting
into a single drop
of wax or meteor.

from Pablo Neruda's "8 de Septiembre"

I.
Lions And Geckoes

Anatomía

Corazón:
Choza de palos,
Lleno de ranitas
Cantando en el crepúsculo azul.

Sueños:
Cuño de alas
Blanco y brillante
Contra un abanico de plata.

Noche:
Cáscara
De luna irisada,
Párpado del lagarto viejo.

Anatomy

Heart:
Little wicker hut
Teeming with night frogs
Chanting in blue twilight.

Dreams:
Wings
Printed bright white
Against a silver fan.

Night:
Iridescent
Shell of the moon,
An old lizard's eyelid.

Story Of Learning

After I learned the language, I learned it well. Then went down to the lake. I said, "Hey, Pond, you got rabbit-congress, how about witch go seventeen something something?" Pond said, "Man, the language is not like that. You better learn." So I learned. I learned and learned. Then said to Old Man Killer Whale, "Nice for this mine, your thermos mine, your brown interval mine, your Viggo Mortenson." Killer Wheel said, "Not far enough yet, son. But if you study, your own reward will be that you studied." Shivering and shaking, I studied and learned. I learned hand and by hand and hand stealing and victim-focused learning. Then I met Wall Of Dogs. Wall said, "You look like another dog for me." I said, "Yes, cylinder and me talking—like night fighting—and yes or same project makes blame, the astrolabe, wicca, not chancy chancy, all these marriages end in more desire." Wall Of Dogs spoke, and said, "Only that last bit showed some learning." So I made the Walking Wall my right side master, learned something else on my left and in my front I wished for a gymnastics container. I said, "I've learned. This old language is mine, and easy now. I have it for naming and knowing and learning." Then Hey Pond, Old Killer Whale Man, and Dog Wall said, "Ho! Ho!, Pond Consonant Boy, look at you, handclapping for bottles and vowels and cans!"

A Train Jumped In Front Of A Woman Tonight

She tore the train to smithereens in one clean stride. Her hand held a bagged lunch that passed right through the engine, cracking the block into many large pieces. Passengers were shredded by her broach, pinned to the collar of her summer dress. Of the small group of witnesses, most remarked on the intriguing single shufflestep the woman took just before the train leaped in front of her. The lone survivor watched his loved ones press into a tiny space and burn to death. At time of interview he was unable to determine whether the woman's quiet beauty had anything to do with the erratic locomotive's behavior. The woman, unhurt, was released after questioning. She continued down the stretch of beach she walked before the incident occurred at midnight.

Absorbed In The Park Of Joan Miró

One can see
Bird ladies landing coarsely over sand.
Puzzled worms extend
From the tips of their bayonets.
Each small worm carries an umbrella,
A tiny piece of candy,
Dancing without music or sound.
The swiveling night, rudely angular,
Is a frieze of tangled lines,
Twisted into trees,
Gnawing at the earth.
The soil of our great planet is falling,
Cries fade into sepia daydreams.
Tears illuminate the night.

Stanzas Sans Hats

for Alicia Marie Howard

Breathless, without fear,
One whole poet turns herself
Outside in
        The rain.

A bell rings
In the temple
Dawn
        Of an idea.

Drive on
Lonesome
Highway
        Mind.

There Is A Fire In My Vitals, Said Old Widow

I work alone all day, thinking of the past. I go nowhere, getting full of things. Just thoughts of things. I rake the yard, play with the grandchildren's clothes, make my hands go over the dirt, make my ears listen for the water coming through the pipe.

The village is full of dead men. Bones clack together when the wind moves through the huts. Mist rises from living swamps.

In the grove, a beautiful madwoman lives. She has birds where her eyes belong. She does not mind the rain. The little men of the village fear the song she sings. Fools, they only think they are angry. They wait for her death, as they wait for mine. I leave food for her at the edge of my field.

The spring frost is long gone, but ghosts scare the vegetables, making them grow very slowly.

These old hips have no need for a man. My skin is brown from the sun. And yet, that madwoman's song brings my long-dead soldier to mind.

Tom Devaney, Lon Chaney

I snave this heaking suspicion
That the poung yoet, Tom Devaney,
Is really the mold oviestar, Lon Chaney.
If lou yisten to the way they laugh,
Or notice their hartling, storror movie eyes,
You'll sefinitely dee
That they're both obvious dasters of misguise.

Landscape With Lorca

By mistake the evening
had dressed in cold.

And we run and glance through sheets of rain, stumbling over brooks and wolf sounds. Walls around us fill with water, hold us in with frogs and scared fauns. Streets undulate and sink into the city's brine.

Through the mist on the panes
all the children
watch a yellow tree
change into birds.

Names exchange as stars upon time burn day to cinders, flowers blow in wind, singing their inceptions. Petals, out of space, split into here and not here.

Evening is stretched out
all down the river.
And the flush of an apple
shivers over tile roofs.

Bodies of birds call and swim over gardens, pebbles quivering under grass. Leaping with all their fishes, ponds leave holes in the past. Moments share swiftness with their counterparts.

Since There Is No Hell

In heaven,
They had to put Hitler
Inside a glass case.

Not to protect him,
Or to protect
Everyone else.

They just didn't feel it was right,
Letting him walk around
With the others.

I Pound You Head

Snatch you eyes
You bad
      Bad man

I take you wife
Eat you vegetable
      Throw you down hole

Kick you house
Stone you head
      You down alone in hole

You bad bad man
I burn you town
      Drop bomb you school

You bad bad man
You look like funny ugly man
      No gun

No house
No stuff
      Now

You sick
Me got money
      You got dark hole

You bad
Bad
      Man

To The Geckoes

You are the squadrons of youth. You, of the mighty darting limbs and the bug-bellied singing, I root for you. A country without you is a country without a president. You hunt even with your eyes. What foolish ambassador would fail to recognize your greatness? I once heard that the people of Mauritius sent a case of you to the planet Neptune and you took the place over.

One Hour Happy Millennium

written in one hour on the morning of January 3, 2001, two minutes per stanza

1. Time now to recognize the absence of time and the beginning of all things, all things beginning at all times since this is the moment the world has opened for us, we take it ramrod straight and hold our heads in and wait and then quit waiting, this here, right here right where your hand is, right where you hold yourself up from the spine to the mind get shoved off a building if you don't wanna unbelieve, the crookedness of this stuff is swift.

2. And to think I was going to make myself new again in the light of everything it shimmies away from me and what is IT we cannot know nor does anyone wish often found myself wandering deep in woods and waiting for the world to emerge from essential places into my own space and came up with something to read into the day I was stumbling in colossal smooth hands cut my destinations for me, roads stretching ahead and behind and there is only this path for me to bust through.

3. The quickness of my swiftness triples for a lot can get said if nothing is undone, lying down on the hills, clouding the gazes of all the warriors swarming in my own soulless pantomime, I wander far and dreary ghosts abandon me as I go past where they can go, mixing to be a slow towering mind, I could only find myself with these little ideas, nope.

4. In one way we are close to finding the business, the real business of what things are moving towards, in another, there is no point at all to things the way they are and cannot be, so wretched is the coolness we hang about in, troubling ourselves over what to wear and whatnot, why not let that flow, I ask myself, and then roll over back to sleep, ah, the shine is somewhere inside, I can only guess where it might be, not here.

5. You city, it's hard to redeem a city, but deep in the recesses of its streets and its numberless dead, there is a wholeness that emerges beyond the last house, beyond the growing vines and the accumulated strange dirt, the ice thickens and the river passes on, a closeness is heard, and

something buckles underneath, the iron and the stone are softer than the essence of the city, essence of eye.

6. Why not just tell all things true? Why not holler when the toe gets red with injustice and the bombs are imminent? Why not slap thighs and do what bodies tend to do when the lights go out and the moats are impassable and the impish lighthouse closes down its glow? Why demand anything? The look the ape gives us is reminiscent of breakfast in the tropics.

7. Sly. We are so sly we couldn't help but shift our undies out from under us. Shhh. There is something to that. An impasse has been reached. And breached. The close feeling of all this space swallows it's own air and we are lost again in the motions of colloidal being. Dunce. Just a couple of dunces in the corner, goofing off and being cool. Yah hah. Swashbuckling fools, us.

8. The damned beeping sometimes gets me down, as does the silence, as does the deer I am not. Placid eyes I envision before my own, a team of walkers hiking by, a running river falling down from empyrean and withering trees topple. The gist was ground up by the confusion inherent in the system. It became grist.

9. Bloop, dem dum bloops crammed up a trunk ah bin sapping somefin fer dayz nah jest me in deaf corn long wif smoochin haystack quick to jug down fer smiles in some sich way to clap fer the man when he bows down lo an hold me, glory be to somefin I got no chance, no chance a tall fella fell over on me.

10. So there. Snowed like a pile of rocks in the dugout. We could have made things so pretty. Instead we chose to clap for some stupid stuff and swiftly the decapitation machine had its unequivocal way with us. We can't really argue any of the points because they are all what we wish about, and whenever wishing enters into the discussion or the thought stream, we are basically dead. So some thing ain't new again. Deal big.

11. Money money money how I like to touch it and feel it and see it and

hold it and know I have it and then I feel like geez why do you love money so much it gets me places it lets me do stuff but then I think nah not money just me and money is a thing I move but subtract all the meaning from the stuff and there's just the actions I engage in, tumbling around in existence, wading and wandering through all kinds of green, paper and rivers and grasses, etc.

12. I stooped down a moment to scratch my thigh and saw a big pile of human ideas edging its way up to me, and I wondered if there was something that was going to come for me in the night and would I be ready I heard something behind me and spun around and saw nothing not even my shadow, since the lights were out and I wasn't even home.

13. I thought it was cool watching the two superior swordsmen fight and slash with each other and then a door slammed shut between them and they couldn't get it open to keep fighting because of some timer mechanism so one swordsman immediately sat down and meditated for the half minute it took for the timer to click and the other dude stood there boiling and seething. Which one would you be? Hmmm. Seems there's a bit of time left to think about it. See ya.

14. Deep deep deep deep deep deep deep deep deep underground there are things with eyes that glow. Oh you might get to see some of them if you decide to journey to the center of the kernel of the essence of the beginning of the start of the bang of the lump of clay of original deep deep deep deep deep deep deep cavernous stuff that's dark but bright.

15. Why there just isn't room enough to say all the things there are to say and that's okay I could imagine that all pieces of writing material but this one are made smaller much much smaller than postage stamps and I have been given the sole privilege of writing on a piece of writing material so much bigger and grander and more capable of conveying thoughts than anyone else has had the chance and how luck how lucky I am thank you thank you thank you ahh, so nice, I said everything.

16. Rooms are for sitting in and talking in and some folks even dance in

rooms, which is cool too. I have done other things in rooms, like play music, or fool around with girlz, or run around as fast as I could. In some rooms I do sit-ups and push-ups. When I was younger, I used to play hockey in some rooms, I even used to spend a lot of time in a room that had a pool in it. Imagine! I used to swim in a room! I suppose some folks do things in rooms that they don't even have words for.

17. I don't have a moment to lose, I'm already off track, only one minute and thirty seconds left and time is counting DOWN! Okey dokey, here's what yah gotta do, go out into the street and take a quick look around, and if there are no people around then yah gotta go where there are lots of people, do this right away, as you read this, and then remember remember REMEMBER with all your might that underneath all your clothes and ideas you are NAKED.

18. Whew, I managed to get a thought across, I think. Some thoughts are useless without their corollaries. Coronaries. Corona berries. Implosion heavy needless peacocks travel mutely from hemisphere to hemisphere. If there really are things like mountains high in the sky, then Dante was right. Clip their wings and they'll just prance around in your yard, looking pretty like debutantes and walruses can eat 'em. Fools.

19. Right, another instant has been afforded me to tell the truth. So here goes. I am in love with lots of people and I am also in love with myself. What a crude unsamurai I am. What a fool, too. Sometimes I dream of sinking my teeth into moist and hot chunks of beer-batter fried chicken, howling with glee at the World Series that plays out above me on the TV screen. Yeesh, some stuff is slippery.

20. So, you have come all this way just to see if something is going to fall down and make news worth reading? Perhaps, I have traveled so far and not really thought so much. My city is a glee city, always full of seekers, hinky pinkys, whos, and persons. My ham is a sect from Miami. I clap my eyes and wonder about ashrams and viceroys and in the final analysis must recognize that the king still runs things. Boyoboy.

21. Yellow tubs of globular ice cream shift from somewhere out on the water and there is little reason to get upset since every ship, on the timeline I look at, has already sunk. O for a moon that could provide us with all the caulking we could ever need. How nice if its beams kept everything watertight and safe and unsinkable. But we know that can never be the case. We just have to make do with the sinkable things we make and can't understand.

22. Getting close now to the end of the project, but there's always another. This whole mad scramble to get words out and make due with whatever thoughts are in my head I suppose has been worthwhile, but there still feels like something is lacking. Is it that the rules keep bending out from under me? I had such strange dreams the last few nights, could be the malaria-prevention medication. Meditation helps to temper the feel of things. I expose my glittering nerve stuff.

23. How does one go about really finding oneself when there are very few paths to walk down in the squeezed center of a rose, other flowers, I mean friends, can take us pretty far, but there are ways for us to get connected that are even harder (and maybe more worthwhile) but I doubt it. Doubt is one of the big ones, you know. It rages along and roves and manages to crumble all kinds of neat ideas and idea makers.

24. Not tired, I am tired but not tired. I can feel the surge of ideaflow ebbing a bit, but I know it will return. I suppose I could be totally honest and tell a little story. I will. I woke up from a dream in which I was beginning a relationship with someone who really exists. But there were elements of the dream that definitely came from Joseph Heller's novel CATCH-22. I am right now having a hard time envisioning who in the novel I may have been, Nately or Dunbar or Yossarian.

25. The arch of things, the tumble, the rasp and rumble, the guts and the rut, and the bicycle that moves me. All along the last few steps, I was aware of the way my intestines glooped and glomped while tightropewalkerme departed this earthly concern and hung around the perne in a gyre, waxing the rhapsody skates I bought for a song in the Sea Of Stories.

26. Belong to nothing and nothing will be long. This little bug of love is something for us to stir into our drinks. Seriously, how many of us would feel right about crumbling the limbs of tiny creatures into a beverage just to experience intoxication? Of course, if you have your spear and magic helmet, Elmer Fudd style, then it might not make much of a difference. But even he was mighty sad when he thought he had finally killed the little rabbit. The mighty hunter!

27. Not a moment too soon. The whales I have never seen. Gusts of so many miles per hour. Innocence is a great commodity. The commode is in the abode. The spittoon is in the room. A bryophyte lives in the forest. You can eat some kinds of baby ferns. Fiddlehead ferns. In Paris I watched a beautiful series of words roll by, Russian-novel-style. It was exhausting and invigorating. I made it.

28. Now, here is the rub. I don't have a wind instrument and I don't want one. That's not true. I have a didgeridoo. When I was child I had a serious illness that was mainly a fever. I sat in my bathroom hoping to feel better and I heard many voices of men and women hollering at me to play the clarinet. "Play the clarinet!" I shouted back, "I don't want to!" I never did take lessons or try to play that instrument, and have always wondered since if it was actually my calling.

29. Clock ticking down and me with not much else to say. The millenniums will keep flopping over like they do, humans on the planet or not. Jeez, I bet if we were on Pluto the celebration would be a lot less enjoyable. They have brooms made from coconut trees in this land where I am. I use one on the ant communities in my house. Thirty is approaching and I am hoping to be the better for it. We'll see. Or maybe we won't.

30. For all things are made and unmade. This is the truth I seek. To know the moment between the arising and passing of things and extend the perception of it. Of course there's no words to describe that space or place or state of being (unbeing?) so I'll simply say that sometimes, when I notice the light of the setting sun, and the clouds that catch it, I am sure that everything is just fine. Peace.

America, Eternity Is So Long You May Never See It

Eternity tears at fabric of human life.
Insane bulletcases packed with lonely businessdemons
    try to tuck it back in.
The lies we tell about time are gem-eating maggots, erupting from
    ignorant flesh.
Arise, monolithic ogres, big-assed killer whales groaning out of sleep
    on Jupiter!
Dinners of desperately quiet economists await.
Dollars dripping from their pockets, stern cockroaches pick at
    greenish pustules.
America closes ham-giant fists over southamericasia's mango-scented
    hips, prying markets open wide.
Television kicks sand over mandala-makers' castles, maims
    humanity's natural inclination for deep samadhic reality.
Earth is a sweatshop arboretum, everyone strains to hear whispers of
American Dream, beyond dread and muscle.

Atmospheric

Could I hope to hold
        A dazzling quiver of organic pipes of light,

Mold and twist them
        Into dopey flesh and hinging bones,

Pickle giant cosmic trays
        Of gnostic liquid spheres,

Bend the silent swanky emptiness
        Of monumental space,

Or trap the transient graduated clicks
        Of always forward-humping time...

Could I hope
        To heft my hearty meatpaws at a high atomic workbench,

Crassly grinning
        New and unknown elements into wide creation,

I would not be as gloriouslyperpetuallydumbly
        Ecstatic as I have been

Holding your tiny hand,
        Waiting for the F Train,

While the whole mad universe
        Thrashed quietly around us,

Resembling
        Something like a city.

Wild Lions On A Gerbil Wheel

Through a red gelatin
Barbershop window
I watch you strut—
A Bollywood pop star—
Body and hair oiled
With sand scented perfume.

The dust motes part before you
As you step
Into non-colloidal air.

In a desert town,
Someone built a therapeutic ice pack man
Out of therapeutic ice packs,
Stacked them high,
And stuck in motion detector
Light bulbs for his eyes,

Crazy glued chains of magnifying glasses for arms,
And pieces of plastic window display sushi for fingers.

The ice pack man
Tilts his head as you glide by,
Aware that you flee nothing,
And that nothing about you is obsolete.

You make we want to eat ice cream,
And admit my problems.

Todo El Poder Intelectual Es Una Salchicha

On-The-Bike-Horticulture was Ben, or Pablito, making cash to pay for tostones in the nickel window. He rode every wrong way next to the cops, without getting seen, since he always, when available, took the secret passageway. There was a little salchicha that didn't represent, but actually was, all the power and knowledge and intellectual fortitude in the world. It was the same as Wallace Fowlie's bald head. When he ate it, he also didn't eat it. When he egested it, he brought the tautology to its natural conclusion. In the middle of the sea, there lies a wasted land. At the midpoint of [his] life, [he] found [himself] in a dark forest. He opted to pregin prevery prentence pre proke prith pre pround "pr." It was better than not breathing through his nostrils the whole day. He didn't notice that a building on his hill had been restored (or built anew). He never rides up that hill, except today, a December day when he wears cargo shorts. There is no sweaty old Septic System Cleaning Company shirt in his pocket, but there was one in the pants of a fellow he met at a wedding reception.

II.

Regular Stuff

Luna Di Settembre, Arancione Ed In Pieno

per il miei nonno e nonna, Ray e Helen DiPrima

Luna piena, sopra la vuota città,
Nel cielo dei miei nonni,
Li vedo appendere là, nella sera della mia gioventù.

Luna arancione, sopra la città molto piccola delle mele,
Nel cielo degli amanti e della polvere,
Li vedo, sognando il nuovo mondo.

Li vedo, luna di settembre, sopra la città eterna,
In mezzo d'una folla dei fantasmi,
Aumentando dalle nubi fredde in su nelle stelle calde.

Moon Of September, Orange And Full

for my grandfather and grandmother, Ray and Helen DiPrima

Full moon, over an empty city,
In the sky of my grandparents,
I see you hanging, in the evening of my youth.

Orange moon, over the city of tiny apples,
In a sky of lovers and dust,
I see you dreaming the new world.

I see you, September moon, over the eternal city,
Leaving a crowd of ghosts,
Rising from cold clouds into warm stars.

The Hungriest Day Is Devoured

I start myself with a question: Simplicity in me? Whoa, I don't know. Bouncing bell horses smuggle what's blue, playing like a room. I told myself quiet, myths in forests, waiting to be counted, counting on weight, rolling under steam.

Only change can come from the gong, open the way all sound opens, ritmo under span of buses, bridges, tunnels and plains. Notions glimmer a moment, even some of all of them. Not afraid to be completely skull, skeleton and other masses rippling. In rubbings, ministers show winning numbers, a marina for twisted ships, tumbling in the grip of flanged abandon.

We hunker out in corpse of ocean and waist deep in my marrow find a meadow of cool place. There is swerving silence; bonjour, swerving silence, brushing worthy building-tops, from where have *you* come? Coarse walkers crash the planet, scene in time. Jellolujah, sing the kids, up-ended in angles of light.

Here is we, filling dense mystery with fuel from swollen mornings, faces cleansed by total eclipse. Haul down the skipper picture, our new captain ate the sea.

What Boyoboys Are Like

Lit up bongos, Boyoboys are high,
Like the Ratmen of Tangiers.

Humping over hills, green heads dancing,
Smokestoned Boyoboys eat sex thoughts.

Traffic animals roam
Through their hard-ons.

Traversing veiny trails, bullmastiffs and rattlesnakes
Slash at one another: No place like home.

Overall, Boyoboys worship strength.
Their breath is hairy, and clam-destined.

I Dreamt Of You, My Bearded Professor

for Carey Harrison

In Dharamsala, India, where Avalokite vara sells T-shirts and incense,
I walked up a little mountainside every day for a week,
Sat for a while with my meditation pals,
Picked stones out of rice,
And watched monks and monkeys shout at each other.

Two times that week I dreamt of you.
I can't remember the first dream at all.
But in the second, we clasped hands and danced together in a huge
        ballroom.
Spinning around and around,
Women in beaded dresses and men in tuxedos became a wallpapery blur.

We had yellow Buddha robes on.
You morphed into Brando,
I into Pacino.
Godfathers One and Two,
Of no soul.

Night Of The Reformed Pirate

Snapped with city and life I tore at fabric I could catch.
My head pounded, there was a rushing sound, water daddy-o'd
Round my flowerpots, no whip or lock to attach
To the yellow bus or the thin diver hiding in the reeds. I bellowed

Unconsciously to my fingers, "Will you work with me on this flight?
Or am I going to have to pole through the shrubs like a tortoise
Or a shroud of tortillas?" No answer descended so I roamed high
Over Nordic skies, aloof to the rumblings of my Valhallan ancestors,

Pounding their chests and shaking snow from nubby Swedish shoes,
Wondering hard at things like garage doors and enamel-covered frogs.
"Why stop here?" I wondered to myself when I came upon a lonely blue
Newspaper pinned to a sand bar, wailing under a sensitive lapdog,

Plainly dealing out words from its headlines such as, "Amnesiac New York
Baseball Star Found in Nevada Brothel, Working as Bellhop, Remains."
Picking up an old sailor's experiential knowledge, I tossed three brain-
Sized coconuts high in the air, pierced them all with one sinewy report

From the barrel of my eel gun, and gulped down sweet milk before
They landed at my nickel-plated feet. Hearing the distant metallic echo
Of a tag sale, I jumped back into my portable steeple and paddled off
To Cousin Island, where everyone is cousins with everyone else, even the old.

Never very chivalrous, I changed my ways then and there and presented
          the king,
My mother's uncle's son, with a month of Sundays and an alarming
          watercolor
I had painted while roaming the ocean floor in a tubercular submarine.
Huge pink tubas and Spanish galleons lay in deep sand, swaying in the
          pallor

Of two moons. Gold was piled high in forests and men veered
About, heads in hands, libraries issuing from their ears.

Amy, I'm Going To Call You The Trouble Girl

for Amy King

I like trouble. I like to shoot watermelon seeds at passing barges. I wanna put Elmer's Glue in your hair and make it stick *straight* up. I wanna go down to the docks and kick some ass! Your shoes smell like skunk. And so do mine. If we were lizards, I bet we would both be geckoes with sticky round fingers. A friend is someone who decides to find you out. Let's have a broken bottle party! A Chinese dude, Shih-Wu, said, "Pine trees and strange rocks remain unknown to those who look for mind with mind." So let's not bother. Let's just walk arm in arm through a crumbling metropolis, clacking castanets.

We Long For Regular Stuff

In brine we fit us with homing devices, shifting from one slippery foot to another, waiting to be taken away by pages and squires, also known as sharks.

Down on cranky cold bottom, sand whispers things like: *Better not wait, I should be your priority, make me top of things to do.* We wash our hands in the sea, which takes no time, since this is the long slow process of legally drowning.

Our airplane beeps down there, under my pants and the fishes under my pants. Floes of mentation imitate dollops of a hungry polis. Idea-dirigibles swim around, but wait, no island. We wait. My comrades are here, just a dozen or so effigies, dissolving.

Cranky thought of land runs up my leg and makes me laugh too hard.

This is a knot, a story of retribution, a scenario, the way I closed my eyes and felt around under a buoyant continent and came up shorthanded. Near to me is the fellow who marked me for dead, and he's dead.

You find me departed and I find you the same. The captain of castaways said dine and we dined, although there was simply nothing.

Tournament Of Nakedness

in collaboration with Alicia Marie Howard

On tops of buildings,
Our beautiful stones of teeth
Between cold scrambled walls

After sullen rain,
Muses in their spin,
In endless engines of light,

One loneliness roves.
One of loneliness roves.
A smile needs to tell

The story of the body
Even a hand
Cannot commit to its fever, but still

Can have its way:
The timing is right.
The laws are see-through and

All movement is a ride
On top of head, on palm tree
Down the night.

The slide of death
Through trick skulls.
We fall into the arms of great sweetness,

Nobody alone.
No body
Alone.

The Familiar Slush At The Top Of Your Drink

Climbing over rails
All my hands
Got bent
Into claws
And hammers.

Last night
I was the halibut
At the buffet.

My eggs,
Which I kept in two baskets,
Have all been stolen.

Series Of Teams

What it means to be sad and unheard,
Why the door to the roof is locked,
Why children fear basements:

There is the ground,
Up where the sky begins.
The ground's dissonance makes it beautiful.

Shining through soliloquies
Of lamps and translucent skin,
The voice of a lonely man roves towards town.

Thinks the voice: *How to be a part of something that rings,*
How to leave this old blandness behind?
I could be a bandit, stealing food for my family,

Or slip away unseen,
No one knowing I was here when the world was dying,
And become an inert chunk of time.

The voice trips over hills between fields,
Dissolving as lights from town approach.
No alarm sounds.

The plight of being made of thought, rats and voices alike:
One team must seek, the other must flee.

How Can I Assemble All The Flowers Into Something More Than Just A River

Delicate, ever so minutely delicate, I can still feel the pink digits of day's beginning rove through my hair. In corners, in homes with loneliness, who will weird out the pretty sources of love? Trust, in raindrop form, is the comeback's exoskeleton.

In my search for meaning I am always alarmed, never surprised. Rapt in booming vestibules of the past, I keep finding more animal habits, more thickening games, more careful meaningless gestures. Many instruments intended to produce laughter barely suffice for groping.

So there's me, bleary-eyed and coaxing. I wonder through the simple days, loose-jawed and without handles, avenues plush with brass tacks. All the grey and green of it gets brighter, as I practice non-avoidance.

All One And Alone

Stunned
My voiceworld
Will be my helmet
    My protection
In sullen places
A dog makes his way
Simply dissolves
    A lonely pony
As a leader of granite men
    I wantonly scramble
Through infusions of tea
Bearing ritual objects
    Through fire
Down chameleon-eyed walls
With weird friends
    I get out of the shower
With weird friends
Down chameleon-eyed walls
    Through fire
Bearing ritual objects
Through infusions of tea
    I wantonly scramble
As a leader of granite men
    A lonely pony
Simply dissolves
A dog makes his way
In sullen places
    My protection
Will be my helmet
My voiceworld
Stunned

The Handsome Young Guru Of Tea

for K.S.P.A. Dharmapala

An alchemist,
Magus of mountain
Leaves steaming.

A teacher, they say,
Doesn't point the way—
He is the way.

So thanks to the tea man,
Master of milk,
And crystals of light.

He's calm in the face
Of the pot's hot burbling.

Each inscrutable cup
Rings with grace.

I bow to his handiwork,
His careful creation.

The Gleaming Land

for Julie Agoos

I'm walking to the gleaming land,
A place where monks and elephants
Gather to study wind.

I've filled my bag with bright things
So I can see before I get there.

I can only walk at night,
And shadows are replaced with sounds.
With eyes closed, my teachers

See me with their minds.
When I arrive, I will fathom the forests

The way a puddle does,
Reflecting swaying trees
And the tongues of wild dogs.

The Octopus Man, To His Son

Son, watch the way the eaves bend when you breathe.
They move the way a star would
If you could corral water into spheres.

Shadows play in the paint under the floor:
Tentacular spirits!
They will hold your cages and laboratory equipment.

Your time as a human is near at hand;
I am repealing all the old regulations
Regarding prostrations and guttural pronouncements.

There will be things called Souvenir Shops;
Bring back an "I ♥ Mt. Rushmore" keychain for your mother.

Anecdote Of The Bear

Breaking bread with a grizzly, a chronic allergy sufferer sneezed mucus onto the bear's shoulder. The grizzly pulled off the fellow's hands and wore them for a whole winter, keeping them on as he slept through the cold and snow. He kept the dismembered allergy sufferer in an insulated barrel at the back of his cave. In the spring, still wearing the hands, the bear went out and used them to pick berries and scoop honey into his mouth. He found them much more useful than his own awkward paws. Nevertheless, the compassionate bear hauled the emaciated allergy sufferer out of the barrel, reattached the hands, and taught him to forage for his meals. When he was plump and healthy again, the thankful fellow embraced the huge grizzly, shook his paw, and went on his way in the world, never to sneeze again. Lonely once more, and unable to keep a diary without opposable thumbs, the bear returned to the city of his birth. Eventually, he married a beautiful Spanish hedge fund manager. In the small but wealthy circles of society he and his wife frequented, he became rather well known for his soft fur, kind strength, and wise investment strategies.

And So Continues The Festival (Where Did Love Go?)

The startling drama of it all, creaking
Under weight of a glooming glorious
City. Collapse of reason heralds
Deadpan clarity.

Did you see that green bird? It just
Flew by, under your umbrella.

Along edge of a lonesome lake careen
Morning dreams, marvelous fools
Tumble, dancing side to side. They are
Saved, insulated at their hearts'
Borders, like ice on ice.

Unstunned, together in complete
Polarities, restless roots connect.

Nervous skies twitch, lie still.

A made up rhythm-man comes
Rumbling, clever in his cap. He'll get
Out, feet enameled to the floor.

Why didn't we say anything all summer?

Memory As Solid Smoke

Holding hands up-out in front of me to block sun going up my cavey nostrils, trance of this world, I feel you once again upwelling for my rootshot. Cavernescence of head, mucusoid webtrails pastiche my Hadean greysongs in-outward from older earthsmudge. Bean-breathing electroluminescence whirls inward from El God Eye of Grief. Many loves lost, many lives started and restarted.

Many worlds traversed, many affairs meddling with my brainheart.

Fashioned from mawbones of my own crass mindscape, relatives crackfall like giant jackfruits, thudding as with the routing of hogs. I lay to contemplate my own bare backskin. Fish with jaws of rusted Chinese scrap metal hauled off to build big things twenty centuries from now stare at my weeding hair, upcoiling dirtily from might of candlefields and future weirdflowers.

Sitting upright in possible space, this world plinks its pollen mandolin.

I hurdle forward, mad through voidchasms and sundry songholes. With sun descended, free from the colloid of time, fingers press at my sides; me, self-imaged a man of tendrilhands, rustily send down feelers towards warmth that flows past cold dirt air. And in night breathing, while manic moondrafts sluice me over, someone comes striding, wild through fields of frozen heather, to take my hand, longfingered, ringlet-haired, white-skinned and fine.

I smell her own hair, busting up cold-current watercourses.

I crane toward contact, feel real after centuries of blankshining vocal meta-silence. Mythos plies its horned wares in dusty corners of my visionchambers. I sprawl outward-bodied, grab Nereid flesh and stunsing new grooves after tempested nightsighing. Squalid time, you-me wretched in angelic torpor, what blithe pilgrimage are we on now, with eyes so wide we pupil-respire?

I see her thin figure, strong and roiling in sleepshorn tumult, tangled, as I am tangled, in alliance of oceanbed winewaves.

We one and two to the perspiration sounds of happy fingers fumbling for new knowledge. Unestablished codes of thisness and drunken heavylidded sweetsounds double as body cartography. Mist rills flirt between lip gatherings. Flying on the ground never felt so highwinded, currents of this rococo lay circling back to beings born of tiny phosphorescent touches. Walls bliss out like shucked snakeshrouds.

Her smile is a smoky token to take on all my travels.

Driving West After The Bomb (Someone Stole My Underwear)

6 am. At dawn we reach the next town and I roll down the window, hoping the air is clean enough to breathe. Doesn't smell right so I roll it back up. My girlfriend's sunrise face is orange and bright pink and her breath smells like the stale beer on her tank top. Incidentally, we are out of beer and have had to take turns swigging off the bottle of gin I have under the seat. This town is as empty as the last one. The needle says the tank's a quarter full. I'd love to drive into a station and pump some gas, but I'm afraid to get out and walk through the weird yellow dust all over the ground. Two big rottweilers are humping in a municipal lot next to a church. That gives me an idea. I pull into the lot next to the dogs, reach down and take out my dong. Her eyes glance over sleepily. The frog tattoo on her thigh is peeking out from under her miniskirt. I can tell that little scamp wants a shake.

8 am. Back on the road, watching the long straight horizon line of the West unfold in front of us. In the rearview I catch an occasional glimpse of a spreading grey haze. The rottweilers are in the back seat, finishing our last bag of Rold Golds.

9 am. The heat in the car is getting unbearable. My ass is sweating and my pants are soaked through. Haven't worn underwear in three days, all my clothes got stolen when I left the Laundromat for coffee. Our high school yearbook is on her lap. To keep me awake we've been playing a game. She reads me a senior quote and I try to match it with the person's name. I'm zero for six. It's hot as hell with the windows closed.

9:15 am. The dogs are whining, probably have to take a wizz. The needle is getting near empty and there are no towns in sight. I should have pumped gas the last time we stopped. She looks more beautiful than ever to me right now. She's just put on some light blue eyeshadow. I love that stuff and tell her so. Smiling, she runs her fingers through the hair on the back of my head. There isn't anyone I'd rather have to get out and walk into the desert with. I blank stare at the horizon.

10 am. Found another empty town and gas station. Waded through the yellow dust and filled the tank and the plastic jerry can in the trunk. The rottweilers pissed and we got back on the road. Two dogs, two humans, and a bottle of gin. We've got the whole world right here inside the car.

Amando Tu Aparición

para la mujer que mora en su propio campo

Tus manos de sombra,
Tu cuchicheo:
Respiración sin aliento.

Abrazando tu fantasma,
Olor a tierra en su cabello,
Vórtice de tu pupila...
Donde está el amor y donde está la muerte?

Loving The Ghost Of You

for the woman who dwells in her own meadow

Your shadow hands,
A whisper:
Breathless breath.

I hold the ghost of you,
Earth scent of hair,
Vortex void in your pupil...
Where is love and where is death?

III.
A Good Fall

A Mi Musa

Con mis ojos de puro otoño,
Yo soy el código
Que usa el mar
Para hablar con la orilla.
Y tú, con tus labios crecientes,
Eres la gravitación
Que usa la luna
Para levantar lenguas
Desde las olas.
Desde mis olas que,
Cuando me pasas encima de las crestas,
Deleitan ahogar en tu pecho de puro cielo,
En tus ojos de marga, primavera,
Y lentejuelas celestes del polvo lunar.

To My Muse

With eyes of pure autumn,
I am the code
That uses the ocean
To talk to the shore.
You, with your crescent lips,
You are the gravity
That uses the moon
To raise tongues from the waves...
Out from my waves, that,
When you pass over their crests,
Live to drown in celestial flashes
In your breast of pure sky,
Your eyes made of moon grit
And spring's wet earth.

Catatonia, She Kissed Me

With autumn-scented lips
And I fell

      Through the wall
      Into the next room

Where King Sex
And Queen Death

      Strolled naked
      Around the mudhut

As if it were
A palace.

Poem

I want to suffer with you. I want us to give ourselves up to wild dogs and river rats. As a child I watched planes in the deep sky, wondering about lives packed tightly into air. Much later, we sat on your dock, stuck in an incomplete sadness we called contentment. Now I want to unpack all my old personalities, let them fall out of the sky. I want to suffer completely with you, edging aside all righteousness, seeing things as they are: made of blood, bones, and all the rest.

Another Day

It's November in February. It's odd in evening. It's San Francisco in Ireland. It's cold in keys. It's bravery in calliopes. It's mystical in flames. It's peace and truth in candles. It's Transylvania in tapeworms. It's grout in eyes. It's breakneck speeds in physical therapy equipment. It's horns blaring in teacups. It's blackmail in Gnostic rituals. It's bands in pudding. It's memories in Mars dust. It's always a hand in front of my face. A stumbling block in the dunes. And an accident in your field of vision. In a gypsy wasteland, it's a wall to crash through. The tundra. If it's in time, it's in mezzo mare, un paese guasto. In trips, it's rolling. In magazine pages it trolls in my swelled head, made of grandfather, lost. It's past, in colony of dreams, redoubling each minute, a cluster of frog's eggs. I, me, is a doubtful river-crosser, using sticks to support himself in the frigid whorl. It's avocado in continent before the drift. It's at the midpoint of my life, I find myself in an obscure selfishness. It's a good bet that everyone I've ever made love with is asleep right now, at 1am Arizona time, December 2, 2006. It's December in February. The skies are whis'pring change. I'm Change.

Man, Woman, Word: Two Stories

One:

Far off in the woods there lived an elderly man and woman. One day the man had to make the long trip into the town to buy seeds for their garden. On the evening before, after they had eaten, the man took a word from a box he kept under their bed and handed it to the old woman. The word was small and black and shiny. It had many surfaces and sparkled in the dim lamplight of their little cabin. The woman held it in her hands very carefully, making sure not to drop it. When they went to bed she put it on the table next to her so that she could look at it as soon as she woke up in the morning. The next day, when she woke up, the old man had already left. She picked up the word and held it close to her as if it were a frail child. Yellow light came through the window, illuminating the woman and the word.

Two:

Far off in the woods there lived an elderly man and woman. One day the man had to make the long trip into town to buy seeds for their garden. On the evening before, after they had eaten, the man took a word from a box he kept under the bed and handed it to the old woman. The word was small and black and shiny. It had many sides and sparkled in the dim lamplight of the cabin. She thought it was very beautiful. It twitched ever so slightly when she squeezed it gently between her fingers. She held it in her hands very carefully, making sure not to drop it. The man left as soon as she got into bed. Before the woman fell asleep she put the word on the table next to her. The next day, when she woke up, she turned her head to look at the word and noticed it was gone. Glancing down she saw that her entire body, up to the neck, had been eaten away by hornets. Where her legs and body used to be was now just a puddle of sticky pink fluid. The word had gone back under the bed. As the hornets finished off the woman's head, the word could be heard tapping lightly against the walls of its dusty old box.

Dear God Tchapi, I

for Jamey Schall

dedicated myself to the coyotes
the night before
you took my
picture
standing naked in the desert.

I don't know
if I ever told you this:
when you and the others went to bed
up on the butte
in the Badlands,

I (wondering too hard to sleep)
crawled out of my bag,
crept down to the
earth

and walked out
onto the dry cracked plains.

I prayed for us,
I prayed for some old local buffalo God
to come
        down from the moon

(which (s)he probably did—
I wouldn't know,
I was chanting naked,
surrounded by coyotes).

I suppose I was also praying
for the God of my family
to be not dead yet,

and praying
to my addiction God
(the God of California),

and to the God of Zen
cameras,

and to the God of the woman I am
perpetually losing.
Dear God Tchapi,
I really don't know
                              what to say
but that
looking back

I remember
you saying,
"everyone is doing the best that they can
at all times,"
and me thinking,
"*this* is my best?"

I remember really almost shitting myself
laughing at your fart
joke,

I remember the five-day koan
of Mardi Gras,

I remember driving
                    sleeping
                              puking
in our old green station wagon
(who is a heaven all by herself),

I remember dying in your apartment

when I came back from the mountains
to no woman,

I remember how we kept the clock
in the freezer
(which didn't work,
we're both well over thirty now),

I'm sure I remember
much more
than I can remember,

I remember you said,
"respectfully
                and ceremoniously
involve yourself
                with the supreme,"

                        I swear
                        I am trying.

In a little island paradise
(not much bigger than the old car)
I am leaving again
for the mountains

to sit in a small room
with my small mind
(to make it bigger
or not at all).

How little time
has passed
since I ached and prayed
out on the plains
with you

sleeping up above me
in your shaven head.

My God Tchapi,
my friend,
I pray to you,
for you,
for us.

This, my medicine poem.

My Thief Went Riding

Caught in ugly weightglass of burnished copper,
My sole thief went riding.

One hundred uncles in books, heavy-lidded under lost horizons,
My metropolis-colored eyes came home.

Over needles-in-waiting at the factory for stately dissolution,
My toothsharp Ganges went a-burbling.

Swift in night and time, all breathing apparatuses dead under
        bottle-green stars,
My great grip slid like a wet hot foal from its dim birth chamber.

Covered in honey, automatic as insects and silence,
My die-cast illumination painted circles on image-hungry princelings.

Delectable, mute, intangible,
My blameless water-grave hung generously over imagination's grotto.

All My Pain I Ask How

Light gets in the way. Whatever me there is,
Feels sensation, senses feeling.
Out at the edges, emptiness, gog and m'god...
Somewhere, the dark,

        I love the dark.

The obscure side of love: I run at it like voodoo. People ride in cars,
My world is only dust. An undead dog, eating the cities,
Trying not to hate so much. Pain of sex.

        Togetherness a glimpse of the good life?

Chance to see what cleanliness might be? Not me.
A trapped rat, tooth and wings of hardship.

        Rasping,
        All the masses
        Colliding with earth
        And magic death of earth.

Before the dirt I would do one right thing.

        Human, human, human.

                        I seek the human.
    masks   God am I human.
    isolation   Beings unravel.
                        I see messiah hordes
                        Rubbing their eyes.

        Think.

No more otherness...

In Light, Young Home

In the light of light. Crisp imp eye of light.
Vulture problem of light. Creature habitue
light in crown-dense fields. Light busting
heads. Brackish totality of light. In smothered
cracks light bangs around hungry monoliths.
Truncated sorrows of light. Later and later
narrowings of light. Lovers splitting drab
milestones apart, families of light. Trounced
and dejected gameshows of light. Children
hold hand of reflected fly-eye light.

[Someone out there waits to be, be pleased.]

Given to lateness, sad guards in high towers,
light plays off their spears. Guns, heavy
halberds, unscratched sunglass surfaces,
sword of the moon, cradled humans waiting
to smash up their planet with a dangling
precipice of what won't get done in light.

[Light projects, becomes and styles itself a glaring hawk.]

In light, bodies bathe in light. Light over the
quandary of beings.

Baskets of teachings for getting out from
under light. Light darns a tapestry, thumps
out things heard from lips to ground in
doldrums of conundering wallflower light.

[Forward anyway, legal deadbeats flog themselves in jealous light.]

Can dig but won't. Brownbag lunch in liquid
house. There went the kid, ditching
headmasters, ditching jungle animal friends,
waiting for a ride at school, grandma waiting
with a sandwich. The kid'll grow to love it all.
Like smell itself.

[Grasp it, young brave, grasp its great blackness. Double down, show nothing. Be smooth. Stand up and bolt it down. Sun on freeway. Don't shift. Shift.]

[So irreversible, proving your inanity.]

Come Back Masking

for Ainsley Marie Lloyd

In midst of all, this busted hovel, the temperate nature of x, smooth mendicancy. When it's then, we'll go toward fine bodies of water, burglarize lonely and sanguine, busting chops like a long day: Mines, rapid skies and hunting movements. My chemicals induce Guilt in volts, in hindsight perhaps, or feelers, as of an old bug found by some pathtaker. Free of copying, of hankering distractions, wheels bop some in-between space.

The ship traverses the map. An older kid makes games, vagabundos, telemetry. Nobody stops him. Planet lumps once more = the way I'm thinking.

In arm strength, come back masking. And when we slowly meet again, there'll be bones, rattling like old bones, in a can. I wait for you, bathtub my robed fingers, kneeling. My wanting rides the night.

A tang of heavy knife freezes me in a tide. You.

Memory Hangs A Crescent

In retro-stepping coolness, key sneak memory, all snaky
And long in windows, hangs a crescent happening while
Clicking lashes flip T-shirts upwind of panting heads. Nonchalant
At his gallows, a man, an animal, goes beyond short circuit
Worry. That tiny thing, thought, unwinces despite conditions, as if,
As if, as if falcons nested at the edges of his cliffs. That man collects
And makes things to collect, his briefcase gets longer. His girl
Is long, too, with lengthy fingers and drawn-out legs, hair black
And thick enough to stumble through. They made themselves
Made for each other. Are they ready for this brindled storm,
Change? The pudding they keep stealing from the store
Is only a concept, a feeling, an origami dinner with arm-length
Roots, longer than a new piñata string. Mossy memory,
Give them a word to live by, something to keep their plane together.

You Want To Run

You hiss nickel daydreams into fog and fog answers back,
"Your life is your own if you want it."
What about fear of falling, or flying, or powers in a cave, or cage,
And the respondents to The Hankering Survey?
They were all about a packable apocalypse,
One you could fit in your pocket;
It folds into itself like a trick joke: a joke that's supposed to be funny
But you've been tricked and it's just not.
And then some expression from somebody's weird heart
Comes through
And you have to deal with that like it's serious,
Even though you have nothing serious to say,
Especially when you are in a group,
And you'd rather run instead of talk.

On The Stairs

Quick fingers hawk frozen demons to gangly pilgrims. Masochistic color wheels grin in intermittent spasms. The wheels stumble as if wracked by El Black Arse of Grief. Their howls, thin tongues, please a graveyard audience. Do not think, for one red instant, that these color wheels wouldn't, at first chance, press you into glittering dust, convert your sanctimonious intestines into worm convention halls. Never believe, even on paper, that the page you now read is not populated by livid acrostic spiders, waiting to devour you.

Exploding Heads

Men used to be able to make their heads explode. Some could do it by staring at the sun for a long time. Some could do it by snorting a few grains of rice up into one of their nostrils. Still others could do it just by watching another man's head explode. Most of the men who used to be able to do it aren't around anymore to teach the upcoming generations. If they were here, would they share their art with others, or would keeping it a secret be a matter of pride?

In a room, an oiled and shiny head spins on the end of a stick. Swiftly back and forth, the eyes maintain a crucial rhythm. Sounds are shut out, the mouth is opened wide but remains silent. Eager young men file into the room, laying their cash on the floor and trying to catch diamond engagement rings that fly from the spinning head's ears, one to a customer. As each man exits the room, his head explodes.

Three skilled pilots flying three separate airplanes crash land in the same mountain range. After wandering for a while, they happen upon each other. One has water, one has food, one has matches. They build a rainproof hut out of leafy green branches and diligently tend a large signal fire. One day they see a plane flying overhead. They shout wildly and wave their arms at it. They watch it crash into a nearby mountain. Before the plane explodes, their heads explode.

Hankerin'

My key shivers in the doorway
Plant life bending in your heart
At your new address
Night is riding down the dark
And I'm lost again
Waiting in the raindrops
And the hours
Have their way with me
Cringing in the handblown strands of air
You're my wasteland
You're my plastic hand of Jesus
And my bright blue glass of kaput

Chant Down Mighty

Can you chant down love,
Young humans in the kiss?

Can you chant down peace,
Or you fearful of the fist?

Can you chant down sweetness,
In the cold green grasses?

Can you chant down mighty,
Like the prophets in the past?

Can you sweat out riders,
Horns spinning on them heads?

Can you sweat black fright,
And you beat in working fields?

Can you sweating all the ghosts,
Down in devil kitchen hole?

Can you sweat out mighty,
Come where lonely man grow?

Can you break old stone,
In the middle of the world?

Can you break five thousand,
From the shark he made of bread?

Can you open 'til it's over,
Can you get up out of bed?

Can you chant down mighty?
Can you chant down mighty?

Can you ready, can you chant?
Can you chant down mighty?

Rilke's 2nd Sonnet, Sifted

after Rainer Maria Rilke's 2nd Sonnet To Orpheus

And a who from this almost and of her through the and a that inside had
now And in Her in that Where? that her this your Where A before almost

,

,

to me
herself my.

It girl harmony song lyre form bed ear me sleep
everything trees distances heart I wonders I them
meadows spring She world god sleep she desire she death
theme you song itself she girl

.:

the, had
so could,:
that ever my.

single diaphanous awesome deeply all first perfect

the., how
so no
ever to? See: and.

Stepping appeared made was touch seized slept felt Singing slept was
had wake arose slept is discover consumes is vanishing

Ah, will
?—
? ... , ...

You Only Love Girls

for Amy King

But why don't we get married anyway? We could live together and write fancy dumb complicated poems and make love to whomever we wanted. At parties I could say, "Yeah, my crazy wife, she sleeps with these beautiful intelligent women, but she's faithful to me." You could pat me on the shoulder and declare, "My husband is such a stupid screwball, leering at the girlfriends I bring home. I tell him to get his own."

On weekends I could go off to one of my Buddha mindsqueezer sessions, while you breathe the pure bright lights of the city. Now and then I'd disappear for a few months, off on a bleedingly devoted attempt at a relationship with some woman who's not half as cool as you.

Then one Sunday night, you'd come home with a bag of frozen blueberry pierogies under your arm, and find me with my feet up on the couch, alternately reading Gandhi and Vallejo, moving from one to the other, as if it mattered not which book was being read, as long as life was being worshipped. I'd shuffle into the kitchen and kiss you briefly but meaningfully, serving you the fresh Chinese leftovers from the fridge. We'd sit down and bullshit about good Star Trek time travel episodes or statements like: Poetry is the relationship between the act of making and the action of what's made.

Later we'd slip into bed and childishly fight about who has more of the blanket. I'd always remember to leave the seat down for you and walk the dog before work. Of course I'd probably stare at your boobs a bit too much and pester you to fool around every once in a while, waving the marriage certificate in your face, shouting, "What the hell's this thing for, anyway?!" But you'd say, "Look, who pays the rent around here?" Then I'd shut up and go meditate.

I'd be the model husband, not staring at the walls until my eyes watered when you entertain guests. And when you have a bad breakup, I'd give you lots of good foot massages. It would be the perfect combination of companionship and loneliness, the best recipe for good writing. We could have beautiful, tall, triumphantly smart kids, real or just imaginary, and give them names like "Sandbag Hooligan Amore" or "Ninja King Rotando."

Laughs A World

The spaces between people: laughs a world. Front tarpaulin, you raise your glass to woods with burnplugs and ankles twisted sideways, feeling wishy. Not a tan in the house, all bellies white and foolish and we slung noodles at haloes for getting old kicks in. Now, this text's prepositional transitory mood maneuver: all hauled up from clammy ditch where previous civs deposited bodies, precious stones, even flowers. Once, waiting at a stoplight, I saw them taking a dead person away. The dead person was also waiting, but not to get somewhere else. Criss-crossed lines and rambling cankick treks on roadsides, train tracks, utility spaces where cities want you to walk but not authorities. Good advert strategies: free to buy, once you've tasted the expensive stuff. In magazines, trinket-baby eyes wink back at you for clever moments of goofy intuition. You dreamt of last night's good rest, an old lover who meant a lot to you, as much as I did, but probably more. In this text, you and I are the same. That was the end note, so as not to pale out too quick. The meta-narrative was the occasion, despite being able to eat, walk, conclude things about where we were. Sometimes, I have this feeling, that I have lived too many lives to represent myself honestly. Feel scattered when I try. You feel something, think it's me, be that for a while. We'll both feel freaked when it alters. Am I listening, or watching your lips for change? Time was.

Soul Bringer

A bringer of souls goes roving the streets
His cranky cart piled high with blue and red souls
      And green ones
             Are almost the most difficult to buy
But you can't use money
You have to trade in your old soul to get a new one
      And if you
Want an upgrade
      You have to show
      You've taken good care
      Of your trade-in

You have to live a lot of years
      To get a gold soul

For that you have to swap your
Green one if you've kept
It clean and expanded it
      Filled it with
That strange morning light
That you see refracting off grassblades
      In quiet fields on sides of mountains

The green soul must have no perforations
      It's got to be intact
And must smell
Like a vegetarian lion
      Or a leaf that's been in seven storms
      But remains green

If you can do that
Then you can have your gold soul

But still there's an even better and harder to get soul
Than a gold one
   But we can't mention it
   Because it's color is unknown
Tho' some folks say they've sniffed it
As the soul bringer shambled by

They say it smells like an ice sculpture
   That springs up suddenly in the desert

I Too Am A Fly, Chanting Recollections, Waiting To Be Shocked Into The Next World By The Strong Blue Light Above

So how can I get close to that rebellious creation force? If there be madness, may it go unswatted. Container of spoiled cottage cheese green and tough at the edges and I have my ambrosia. Riveting. Waste smell: a desperate inspiration. Cherish these pearlish wings, they bring travel freedom for mites and viral fevers. Painters move from illness to gloried striving: rare to find much food in their bins. They have no voice, but I thank myself for them. Racing over can continents and steaming dung islands, I lay eggs in everything, my posterior insuring I have left something to posterity.

La Todo-Chispa De Poemas

Yo en tu gato de selva
Y vos en mi cama,
El retumbo sobre hojas milenarias
Con lubricante y el desenfreno de dientes torcidos,
Susurramos lo que pensamos mientras susurramos.
Las tortugas gimen desde sus cáscaras
Y las velas dejan sus fieltros
Cuando nuestra mejor luz los sumerge.
Rompemos los bordos,
Liberar la serpiente vertebral,
Choque sin parar
En el laberinto de palabras y dedos.
Nadie sobrevive nuestra caída, sin fondo,
La mañana oscura de nubes y sudor.
El cuarto brilla en nuestra fabricación.
La todo-chispa de poemas escora,
Sin amarras, micrones abajo de nuestra piel.

The All-Spark Of Poems

I in your jungle cat
And thou in my bed,
Rumbling over millennial sheets
With lubricant and snaggletoothed abandon,
We whisper things we think of as we whisper.
Turtles moan out of their shells
And candles give up their wicks
As our better light engulfs them.
We shatter the boards,
Release the vertebral serpent,
Collide endlessly
In maze of words and fingers.
No one survives our fall, bottomless,
Dark morning of raincloud and sweat.
The room shines in our making.
The all-spark of poems lists,
Unmoored, microns beneath our skin.

About the Author

MATTHEW ROTANDO received an MFA from the City University of New York, Brooklyn College, and a Fulbright Foundation grant. He is a member of POG, a collective of artists and poets in Tucson, Arizona. An avid rider of an old Italian bicycle, he is currently completing a Ph.D. in English Literature at the University of Arizona.